Caruso for the Children,
& Other Poems

Caruso for the Children,

& Other Poems

by William Dunlop

Rose Alley Press 🌹 Seattle

Published in the United States of America by Rose Alley Press

For information, please write to the publisher:

Rose Alley Press

4203 Brooklyn Avenue NE, #103A
Seattle, WA 98105-5911

Some of these poems have previously been published in
Cambridge Review, *Caret*, *Encounter*, *English*, *London
Magazine, New Statesman*, *Outposts Poetry Quarterly*, *Poetry
Northwest*, *TLS* (*The Times Literary Supplement*), the P.E.N.
anthology *New Poems 1971-2*, and *New Poetry I: An Anthol-
ogy*.

Library of Congress Catalog Card Number: 97-65389

ISBN 0-9651210-2-X

The cover design shows a portion of "The Clock Tower in
the Piazza San Marco" by Canaletto (1697-1768). The
publisher thanks the Nelson-Atkins Museum of Art, Kansas
City, Missouri, for permission to reproduce and display
this image.

Typesetting by Electromind Design
Printed and bound in the United States

For Miranda & Benet & Kate,
and Revelle

Contents

Caruso for the Children,
& Other Poems

THE TREE-RIDER

He was the greenstain boy with barky knees
and heart yo-yoing between throat and boots,
crouched in the highest saddle of a tree

the wind was wild to pluck up by the roots
and whip cartwheeling up into a sky
flustered with clouds like floundering parachutes.

For all its rant and mime of agony,
the tree had stuck its toes in, bobbed and weaved,
a crooked angler all agog to try

to wrap the gale up in its trawl of leaves.
He, at his point of balance, eyes slashed wide,
cheered wind and wood alike, rode the big heaves,

the thresh and bulge, the pulse he sat astride
which was the place, but more a way to be—
you cannot say that he identified

with blast or root, the founded or the free.
From their long grapple neither could decide
he learnt the style of not being satisfied,
a point to perch on, his identity.

WIMBORNE MINSTER

There, on our way to Devon and the sea,
We stopped for lunch. The hulking Minster lay
Bemused by sun, and all the town, that day,
Yellow and soggy, like a pear, with heat.
My father shivers, pushes back his plate,

And freezes Wimborne Minster.
                       An apple core,
A fox's mask, a dead tobacco smell....
The doves brew silence, and a mellow bell
Burdens the air, beats twice. Life, life is short.
Outside, my father lifts a hand to tilt

The brightness from his eyes.
                     Whom should I meet
In Wimborne Minster, if I went there now,
With just that slant of shadow on his brow?

My father cursed the winding coast-road. We
Were on our way to Devon, and the sea.

ONE SEPTEMBER SUNDAY
(3 September 1939)

Lace curtains billow outwards, try to drape him.
His ladder's jammed against the sill. Indoors,
Somebody's left the wireless on: it drifts his way
Thinned to warm air. All talk, no do. He draws
His brush along the lintel square and solid,
And cocks his head and aims the next clean swathe.
The radio goes on murmuring to itself
Like some sick, sad old man....Here goes:
Fresh crimson trim. How bloody stiff he'll be
Tomorrow, God knows; and his nails get clogged
Keeping his hand in. But, in such fair weather—
Sun feathering his back, the way the wind blows—
He loves the work. He wouldn't trade this job.
He'd like to see the painter who'd do better.

MIDLAND AUTUMN

The old house, freshly whitewashed
to make a dying splash,
briefly blood-spattered,
as its last mountain-ash
breaks out in a rash skitter.

Along the curb range
ochre and orange
cars, a ruddy lorry, vans:
one buffer's lemon sponge
rubs up a richer bronze.

Beyond, drab muddy fields:
a brandnew, bandbox yellow
tractor cuts a bold
shadow across the furrows.
Behind, a swell of sallow

woods, hooded in smoky
duns, wan tans.
The sky's turned raw and streaky
where the pines aim to spike
the sun's cold yolk.

Homeward bob crimson shopping-
bags; boys in brilliant blazers,
redbreasted, whistling; Mrs. Croft's mop
of tawny hair; Jane's russet scarf; the Major's
breast plugged with a shocking poppy.

SOUTHAMPTON: 1940

Just such a September—
the flushed air of evening; the blue mist curling
and wreathing the tree-trunks, furling the leaves;
the first star sharp as a pin by the inky steeple.
Black water heaving
sluggish, like oil, in its lip, and suck,
at piling and slipway and jetty;
and the black felt city
over the river, cut close to the sky, breathing
a feathery hush; and the west amazing—
not the freakish blazing
of one night, or two; but all through
just such a September.

How late it stayed light!
—Of so sanguine a timbre,
the sailor's delight
of red sky at nightfall, the jutty
steeple and chimney, the hulk of the city,
and the black river.
And the humming, the throbbing,
not splitting, but brimming
the quiet with their quiet persistence in coming
night after night in the gloaming,
like flock on black flock of the homing
geese, serene, precise,
and in such numbers!
Not five in formation, not fifty,
but the five hundred
German bombers—

The red sky at midnight! The clamor!

BESIDE THE SEASIDE

You wouldn't say that she "submitted." No,
Whatever prompted her was something new
and docile not at all. Perhaps it had to do
with the short turf, the white cliff edge, the slow
cloud promenade, the surge and thud below

as each fresh wave broke down. So, anyway,
touch, tremor, nakedness all made good sense
to her, quite suddenly, and down she lay
and smiled, and helped him to forget the tense
first panic, meeting not the least defense.

And afterwards, she begged a cigarette,
lazed on her back, and beamed back at the blue
sky, blameless. He was dumb. More vehement yet
the sea beat up against the cliffs, and threw
its whopping slogs into a cave that drew

the sinewed swell out of a foaming sleeve
and sucked it in, to—like one heaving block
of quartz—explode: boom hollowly; and leave
in skittery files licksplittling through the rocks,
till the next wave recruited them, and shocked

itself to spume, finding passivity
exceeded penetration. He watched (while she
lay with her skirt around her hips, and smiled
as at a dutiful, obliging child)
and felt the strangest pity for the sea.

GOING WEST

After the black Atlantic, America blazes:
a gold web of coast-roads, pendants and clusters
of valuable towns, the brilliant traces of Boston
falling behind, New York approaching....
Who would think black-out, except
a child of the 'forties, who sips
quick at his drink, hoods the flame of his lighter's
pinch of illumination?

He used to turn chairs into ships; he was sometimes a car,
a puffer-train often: all peaceable transformations,
pile-ups and crashes and wrecks notwithstanding.
But his flights were always a bomber's;
the cities he built were strictly viewed from above,
and marked for destruction. He croons
as the clenched hand coasts over
in a long loving arc, and pinkly unfurls
on target, releases blockbusters.

Poum! he implodes, and coughs, to persuade his neighbor,
or convert himself. A gunmetal voice
desires he extinguish
his smoke. He sits to attention,
cradles briefcase to paunch, settles his glasses;
his hair's thinning out, he's nearing his forties.

Watch out, New York: take cover, Boston.
A child of the 'forties is now
the man of the world.
Wheee... he confides to his cup, and *ka-pow!*
Before he unbuckles his seatbelt,
he should brush the bombs from his hands.

IN MONTANA

My tenth day in America, I found
the place became less funny.   Nothing changed:
our Greyhound lapped the miles reflectively,
and still we ran beside the railroad track
which bore us company, from long time back,
into a future looking just as blank.

Any old novelty thus came to count
for something special.   The spare earth moved to sleekness,
as freshly fledged, beneath a combing wind,
as the first green in Eden.   Once or twice
we passed a shack still flaking off its hinges,
or, in the roadside lurch, a baking car
whose driver had baled out God only knows
how long ago, and left his '50 Olds
marooned in time.   I'd never seen the grass
look just that new, or relicts quite as ageless.

My eyes were being widened.   When I saw
a big fresh sign *Historical Monument:
1900* point to vacant distance
I hardly raised a smile: I looked out, sharper,
to be in time for what was there to see.

RAINIER

one day in seven, roughly, pokes its head
out of wool-gathering, and hogs the sky,
imposing, in the distance, on the eye.
Lo, the poor Indian looked on it as God.

Then duty-bound, correct Vancouver came
and, seeing that it never was divine,
took from a mate its new official name.
I like to see it loom from time to time:
it's picturesque—sometimes, almost, sublime.

SINGLE MINDED

"Well," I say—
For the third time—as pauses
Lengthen, like the shadows outside,
"I'd better be off...."—but I stay
For that one last drink, and savor
How he's getting fatter,
And sip at her prettiness: though, of course, I'd
Want something better.

"Please don't trouble...." I say, but they have
To come to the gate,
Though it's turning colder.
And I turn, at the end of the street,
For my casual, obligatory wave
Just as she snuggles her head
On his chest, and his arm rounds her shoulder.

Not that I'm envious! "Poor chap,"
(I was bound to say) "one saw it coming:
Still, he could do much worse."
And I—think of those all set to come running;
Am I sorry I didn't...?
Just the reverse.

Yet I see them still, as I round the corner,
In the same attitude
And the kiss uncompleted; she lifting her face
As he moves to secure her
In the way man and wife
Flowing back to each other, may turn to exclude
Mere acquaintance from their life.

"Do come again!" she said brightly,
And he chimed, "Any time...."
I might, I suppose, but it's not very likely....
Could they entertain
All my thirstiness? No—
Though not seeking to slight them—
I won't go again.
Until we can invite them.

THE PHOENIX

One flesh, both birds, we stoop. Claws
Pluck at our nape. Who kills, who dies?
In a warm rain
Of feathers, plummeting, I see her eyes
Strain at a favorite surprise
And melt. Flex of her craning neck
Seems set to drain
All savor from the air; a beak
That's soft as flannel delves
Deep, to my very quick. Our pulses stall, and pause.
Clock ticks again. A chink
Of light wanes on her forehead, and we blink
Back to a recollection of ourselves.

A real thrush chirps, outside. O
Fond allusions, lucid similes
Of fowl, and fire,
You lose your relevance, not by degrees,
But in one throb. She says, "You'll freeze...."
And sheets us deftly, as if dead;
Yes: to desire.
One man, one woman, in one bed;
All wooden, now. My lips,
Still mumbling on a random curl, let go.
It leaves an ashen taste.
She sighs, and shifts. I find my hand displaced.
Her mouth looks sooty, charred by the eclipse

Which yet is only passing.
                              Glints
Again, like an awakened eye,
A flaring disc
To play along the curving of her thigh
—That lissom tinder—and supply
A sheen of plumage to the badge
Of nestling down.
Light widens, bridges us, to pledge
And burnish, in our blending,
The sudden bird who, in one strut, will rinse
Lethargy from his wings.
The sparks dance on our throats; he starts to sing
In one unbroken melody, ascending.

VARIANTS OF LOVE

At home, the great philanthropist forgets
His children's birthdays, and confuses names;
Sometimes his study window, shooting up,
Will bellow briefly at their noisier games—
They see his picture in the papers, awed
Beyond laughter that they know he snores.

He brings a book to meals. The children poke
And mutter urgently, buzz like pent flies,
Stare glumly at his incidental jokes:
Their faces pass like motes before his eyes.
Once, a bread-pellet, right off target, burst
Full on his cheek: his hand dismissed the wasp.

But this is the great man: Peace Prize,
Humanitarian, champion of the poor…
And Mozart, too, rapt with his string quartet
(D Minor) while Constanze strove to bear—
"Engage a wet-nurse? Bring him up on water!"
(K. 421.) The child died two months later.

I honor one, and love the other, take
All my best girls to hear *The Magic Flute*
And Universal Love; I load them each
In turn with Pamina's attributes,
And fail to gauge their own. I draw
Away from one to love another more—

Or so I fool myself. Admit it, then, I lack
That seeming distance from my own that tells
Of wider sympathies; but still my heart
Beats time at odds with those engaging bells
Which chime for harmony, to cherish one
And let the rest lapse into dead-and-gone.

And yet, between two stools, I value most
Those individual hands which ease my falls
And try to raise me to them; being so close
To two or three shields me from loving all
In my apartness: that music Mozart tried
To sing himself to rest with, as he died.

WORDS IN THE NIGHT

Night, and hearing
Makes sense again; the air is clearing
And the small sounds sharpen, like stones
Dropped in the snow, which, disappearing,
Still pettily dint
That fragile composure, but by it
Made pertinent.

So words in the night
Fracture the stillness, and enhance it
Along with themselves, as black and white
Bring out the quality in each other,
And the intervening
Silence in speech should discover
An intenser meaning.

Now I could speak
So clear that each syllable would be telling
Tales of the heart; and hear,
As you pause in reply, the silence spelling
Out love, receiving
All the phrases of joy from the mere
Dear sound of your breathing.

But all I am saying
Is: *Isn't it quiet?*—and the words conveying
Far and wide, and no more
Than the howl of a dog compulsively baying
Under the sway of the moon;
Or the blab of the tap; or a far clock striking
The same jumbled chime as at noon.

LOVE DUET

Some—I believe it—find this most pleasing fiction
the stuff of truth: a voice that pulses
conveys the strains of spirit *in excelsis*,
the full heart's purest diction;
and when the strings squeal loudest, brass bombardment
                                        thunders,
true love, they moan, and on that top note founder.

I like it, too, but in a dubious fashion:
great gulps of airs that I sup up inflate
the body's currency; at such high rates,
the poor heart pitches to contrary motions,
churns blood to borscht, and canonizes hormones,
and bellows bravos at its own performance.

And so, my love, switch off that braggart tenor
plighting his troth in full fidelity,
that shrill soprano's billowing high sea
of outrage offered her ambiguous honor—
I love them both, indeed, but to distraction:
your being here concerns my satisfaction.

Love moves by subtler rhythms, and small sounds:
a glass set down, clothes shucked, skins' conversation,
duet of breaths—the orchestration's
conventional enough, but it abounds
in touches of a sheer felicity: catch
in my voice; your chuckle; a struck match.

SILENCES

Some stress the cant of an eyebrow when lovers entirely
accept that each comprehend the other,
but *not*...let us say, her favorite show on the telly,
his Worcestershire sauce, reproduction of Whistler's mother—

unaccountable! And soon, laughing matters. Other pauses
                                                seem simpler:
for instance, it's evening. The normal windows are open.
The view from our room proposes a modest sampler
of backyards and roofs, some appletrees, green hills sloping

away to range vaguely the usual blue mountains beyond.
The sky is mottled with clouds like dangerous bruises.
A blubbering faucet, some child's cry add mites of sound
to the brim of silence summing us up, and our noises,

while the sun simply goes down. We may not lie to
each other, we know this: we are dumb in each other's distress
at all that we share, but would rather not try to,
are not equipped to express.

MR. MOLE ADMITS IMPEDIMENT

Precisely what he had in mind she said
or hummed out loud
the tune that he'd been brewing in his head

and he'd have rendered: she need not have borrowed!
He knew propinquity
of the blind, burrowed flesh, but he was cowed

by this assumption: she took a liberty
in saying *Snap!*
She read his look, disturbed, spelt out that she

could feel herself at fault for some mishap....
A root of suffering's in telepathy.
Together they were pinned: she'd sprung the trap.

It clicked upon him like a thunderclap.

END OF SUMMER: AFTER YASUJIRO OZU

September's here: so what. Trees
Stand sulky, without breeze to shake
The dust from their soured green. The lake
Stays creased, has lost the shimmer
It's worn all summer.
Wasps are a bugger, and the days-old papers
That bat them off report that rape
Is on the rise. A favorite cup
Dives at the kitchen floor. Both pennants are wrapped up.

And grandparents have come, to stay,
Fret, get in the way,
And bribe the kids to know them better.
My wife looks out a tighter sweater
And aims her sharp-edged breasts her mother's way.
Grandfather scores
Our age's laxity, deplores
Disorder. I tell him I hate barbers.
And conversation lapses
                              and all strength is labor.

The children tire, and quarrel, and are pecked,
Too late, to bed. My wife subjects
The nylons she peels off to scrutiny
That has no eyes for me.
We lie, apart, in bed
And hear stray peevish buzzes overhead
And know they talk of us. "You can tell...."
They're taking turns to say, "...not going well...."
And "*I* would say...." and "That's what *I* said."

Ozu would show them smooth worn kimonos,
Squat on their heels, compose
Their hands, and in their silence frame
Words which remain unspoken. All of us would choose
A mode of anguish kinder on the eye:
The rest is all the same
At heart, at least. At least, we try
To live, and fail, at least.
I slide a hand. She clenches up her thigh.
What goes to make a man makes me a beast...?

I climb from bed, and look toward the lake:
A strand of willow prints
Its slender patterns darker on the dark
That keeps the mountain—Fuji, or Rainier?—
Away till dawn restores to it the tints
It's worn for ages. I can hear
The whole house fill up with the quiet breathing
Of old, and young, even
Hers, at last. And now, still later,
The moon spreads out her fan across the water.

INCOMPATIBLES

Somewhere a door slams, and it will again:
I lie on edge, in wait,
And wince before the crash. I strain

My ears against a hum of dust, translate
Each chance remark
That tells of grudging wood, and the wind's ache.

My eyes brim dizzy in the teeming dark;
I have to sham
Dead to the world. Could I but strike a spark

Or breathe a word to tell her where I am!
I cannot rise
But hear an exit line in every slam,

Slam, slam the whopping door supplies—
This has gone on all night. In vain
I long to warm her feet, kiss dry her eyes....

Somewhere outside I hear her as she cries
Against a door that slams, and will again.

PENDANT

The frail thread snaps: pearls scatter.
Hardly a cascade,
and yet the few poor brilliants made
terrible clatter.

And some, still skirling, roll
to deeper hideaways.
Still there are days
when one more bowls

me over, squeaky
beneath my tread;
winks as I make my bed,
knowingly, cheeky.

You say you want no share
in spurious keepsakes, paste:
well, you have taste.
Not all that's rare

is precious. See:
out of a partial light
how dull they are, how slight—
stage jewellery

for a stupid play
that flopped.
Now that the curtain's dropped
for good, I'll cast away

every tricky gem
I took for legal tender.
O, who will render
me free of them?

Glints of memory
still play upon my breast,
where, once or twice, you pressed
radiant, attached to me.

DIVORCING

Lust puffs her face: her sweet breath croons.
Faint music strains from the next room.
The window implicates a moon
Chipped by the shifty fret of leaves.

A silk thing slithers from a chair.
Her thighs with mine combine, and there
Is some commingling of hair:
Her husband's in Los Angeles.

And two breasts set themselves apart
Like those I thought I knew by heart,
My hand is not much moved to chart
The salient alterations.

Brisk clockwork keeps each tick distinct,
Reminds us, crisply, that we think—
Eyes staring upward, hands unlinked—
In terms of separation.

A moth's soft kite clamps to the ceiling:
A curious face there—plaster peeling—
Twists to a parody of feeling
True love, or least resistance.

There is a warping sense of how
Unspeakable questions plague her brow
Senselessly. This will do for now.
Let all this keep this distance.

NEIGHBORS

CARL ERNST

Carl is a big man. With flat blue eyes,
a bulbous belly, frayed suspenders, thighs
like bolsters. He has a wife,
shrewish and small. And one grown daughter, who
takes after him. Fat thighs, eyes flat and blue.

Carl works, likes television, worships force,
permits one brand of beer, prohibits coarse
expressions in his house. He owns two guns,
and his own home; thus, he has certain rights
to honor. Looters he would shoot at sight.

Law has no right to arrogate control
away from him. He grips the blackened bowl
and jabs the pipe-stem to enforce his points.
Respect his property. Define "a mob."
The first man through his gate drops like a dog.

His wife's eyes snap a picture she approves;
his shapeless daughter irons, her face unmoved.
He squints out through a window, aiming at
rickety nights of screeching tires, and shouts
as yet too distant clearly to make out.

Carl sizes up Carl's dark reflection, framed
in the black depthless pool of windowpane.
His wife turns up the television, draws
the blinds, for privacy, or lest Carl dwell
too long on darkness like a wishing-well.

DONNA JAMES

When Donna James was seventeen,
And prettier than now, she dated
A boy her age, shy, amorous,
And ordinary. So, she miscalculated.

She went with Len a month or so,
And let Len drop. And Len became
In three-four years the Lenny Joe
Of stage, screen, and recording fame.

While Donna, straight from high school, wed
Jim James, whom she believed would go
Far. Well, Jim has not done bad:
Made foreman three-four years ago.

They have a cat a kid a car
And color television: when
Jim's home at six, that turns them on
And makes their night, till half-past ten,

With prime time close-up Lenny Joe
Complete with grin, guitar, and girls...
And sponsors who tell Donna how
To junk her curlers, still have curls,

And, with a supermagic bra/
tampon/cola/facial cream,
To make the unjust years roll back, and be
Incorrigibly, seventeen.

FRANK MOSER

Frank has gone underground. Who'll tend
The square of grass Frank kept down to the end?
A squinting, humble man, whose wife was dead
And buried—a real shrew, they said.
He kept indoors all winter; when the trees
Presumed again, you'd see Frank, on his knees,
With head bent low, inquiring of the earth
What had transpired against a plot of turf
Which soon resumed its lustre. What a lawn!
One slab of emerald, and combed, and shorn—
Gum-wrappers Frank would pocket, and stray leaves,
And trespassers spray dead: still, he'd retrieve,
Humbly, some brash kid's ball, and stand, and grieve....

Now Frank's gone underground. "He wasn't proud,"
The neighbors all agreed—at least, allowed.
A little, puzzling man, much like a mole:
You'd say he loved that lawn with all his soul
To see him mow it, wield the careful shears,
And, hatless, blinking—sweat can look like tears—
Watch his new sprinkler raise its wheeling veil,
Fan in the sunlight like a peacock's tail,
All day lay down its soft incessant flail.

BETTY LUSTY

Betty Lusty's on her way—
just the same as yesterday,
slams the car door, pulls away
with a lurch.

Betty Lusty wears hot lips,
black net stockings, heels that trip,
skirts garnished with a flounce of slip
trailing.

Betty Lusty's rouge and lace
do not charm her into grace,
redeem a flat cosmetic face:
she's homely.

Betty Lusty is a laugh.
We say, half-jokingly, and half
something else: "There's Betty off,
again."

Grandfather knew of scarlet women,
Mother would have thought her common,
now we say she's only human:
poor dear Betty!

Where she ventures no-one knows,
nor claims to care, but we suppose
anything we fancy goes
with Betty.

One short suburban block supplies
every old name of quality:
anger, sloth, and avarice
peek through curtains,

and gluttony has learned to slim;
envy and pride are in the swim,
ask all their valued relatives in,
and watch for Betty Lusty.

REX SLATTERY

Through a fine sieve
his sight's trained;
scans over faces
as if snow-blind.
Sparse, ice-blond

hair peaks his brow.
He keeps aloof.
Contempt for these surroundings
Can force his laugh,
a cougar's cough.

If he speaks, plants
words like pitons.
Chimneyless, quick
to clash together curtains,
his house is spartan.

The town holds nothing
to discover.
His ways and means
rope tight together:
no wife, no lover.

Weekends are footholds in
a life of crevices.
Then, he scales above us,
has mountains for mistresses,
friends in high places.

HELEN McBRIDE

Beautiful eyes, in a face turned forty,
yammer for help, for release from the duty
of looking their best till they drive themselves dotty.

Once she roused men as dull as potatoes,
made their eyes bulge: now those good looks turn traitor,
with merely a rooted regard they treat her.

Because his glance showed him at one with her mirror,
she tore at the face of an old admirer:
a cheat and a cheapskate she called him, an error

she was partly glad he found hard to forgive her.
Twenty years back, they had planned their world over.
How could she suffer so seasoned a lover?

Beautiful eyes: all injustices hurt them.
They stand wide with dismay at the patent corruption,
the falling-away that obtains all about them.

PATROLMAN ERICKSEN

He held a buckled hubcap in one hand
and measured skidmarks with an easy eye.
Once he began an undistinguished hum
then checked himself, but seemed indifferent why
a bunch of kids with little else to do
should drive and drink and drink and drive and die.

His name was pinned not too close to the heart,
a pistol hung demurely at his thigh,
the radio chirked and chattered in his car
which winked an unaffected bright blue eye.
He counted bodies off. It was his job
to look and see and judge and write no lie.

He'd say he had no time for poetry.

MIKE YARMOLINSKY

Big, blond, and happy, he looks good
even in confinement,
and innocent of a single glance
at this week's assignment.

What should he care if Anna kills
herself, if Levin marries,
who rushed more than two hundred yards
in thirty-seven carries,

scoring three times? The orthodox
pronounce his All-American name.
I put a case for patronyms:
he thinks I play the weirdest game.

Books dwindle in his huge red hands....
O holy Russia, sacred cow,
your herds and their great teacher are
fully translated here. I plough

such alien furrows that Mike wears
the same (in my conceit) bemused,
sweet, patronizing smile that watched
that mad Count Tolstoy hammer shoes.

A CHANGE OF MOOD

for Ran Hennes

On Second, at Main,
Homesickness calls me. Nothing I could name
Induces it, nothing in sight
Affords me correspondence; even the light
Is clearer, sharper here—yet, all the same,
I feel I might
Be standing where the High Street drifts into Church Lane.

A whisper in my ear—how plangently
It echoes—summons me back,
Proposes to my eyes
How the rank ivy pries
Along the churchyard wall, whose dry
Sandstone peppers the air, and how the black
Frets of the yew-tree pink the evening sky,

And clogs my throat with treacly mustiness
Brewed in the village sweetshop's huge glass-stoppered
                                                    jars....
The humbug of nostalgia!
A police car's
Outrageous hee-haw dins
A block away, displaces my distress
With a live prickling along my skin—
Smalltown, America, swarms right back in

On that insistent note, proclaims
Its vital difference. Nothing to do with names,
Nor sights, smells, even taste; but tone of voice....
Lights switch, and I am shooed
Across, no choice,
From sunned to shady sidewalk, set aflame
By vivid accent, the imperative mood

Of PARK. EAT. DONT WALK. As who might say
Get Rich, Get Smart, Get Lucky—or *Drop Dead.*
Live in the present all the signs convey,
And that invigorates; or stuns.
Where I was bred,
A mild persistence never pressed its claim.
My knife-edge blunted as I scraped away
Moss from the gravestones' perishable names

To help a tourist—some American chap
Hunting forefathers two centuries back.
Later, I walked him down the High Street. Faded blinds
Whispered through dust: *Gents Outfitter & Hatter,
Antiques, Old-Fashioned Teas.* A cross, and plaque,
Recalled *Our Glorious Dead.* And down the wind
The chiming hour spoke softly: "Never mind."
And "No-one's fault." And "In time, nothing matters."

LONDON AIRPORT

How the first shudder and dip
As we veer towards landing
Shatters our pressurized fellow-feeling!

We are all brought down to earth. But for these—
Suddenly—alien folk it is nothing more
Than a jumping-off place, a foot in the antique door

Into Europe. My tread is more wary. Alone,
Stepping into conventional English air,
I feel my skin tighten, and my nostrils flare.

Say the animals served just a term in the zoo,
Which then turned them loose, back where they came from,
Would they not come home

Something like me?—although I
Have enough human pride
Not to be seen trigger-kneed, bug-eyed,

And enjoy few illusions of freedom. But if they
Felt something like joy, so do I. And a new sense of danger,
And the pangs of a hunger

Which may not be satisfied, ever.
Though I smile at the guy
With a camera looped round his neck, wave goodbye

To the girl I sat next to, I'm less civilized
Than they might imagine. Though London has no Central
Park,
And less simple violence, it too can stand for the dark

Bristling, veined with essential intimations
Of terror and love, rank with remembered scents
That teach me how I am haunted, how I must hunt.

ABOVE IT ALL

I stand at her highest window:
Through the burning glass,
London spreads herself for me
As if I owned the place.

She rears up her landmarks to ogle
My glance, attain my nod:
I pinpoint Cleopatra's Needle;
Could spit on Nelson's head.

From this point of vantage
I might be Sherlock Holmes
Probing her devious workings:
It's just like at the films

That let me tell Americans
"Well, goodness, Belgrave Square...."
In the tone, falsely familiar,
Of "Sure, I've slept with her...."

In a different movie
There's a sloppy, dumb
Fellow who lusts for glory,
And runs away from home.

At first he does quite nicely:
One night he billets where
The wife he left behind him
Is the house's top-notch whore.

Such things can happen,
And dislocate a man.
I and my belonging
Might well be on the moon

That, yet to vanish, thinly
Blemishes the air.
Such a diminished presence
Has little business here.

Once—even at the level
Of the street that teems
With dwindled life beneath me—
I lived here. Now, the Thames,

Heavy with litter, crinkled,
Captures my eye, the pin
That shivers on the wrinkling of the water,
And does not prick its skin.

A FACE IN THE CROWD

Who does she remind me of,
That girl?—eyes dark, black hair
With blacker sheen, cut square,
A Sphinx-like look, a Pharaoh's daughter
—And with that thought my memory's caught her,
I almost call out "Clare!"

And she responds, but with a shrug
That says I've stared enough,
Then bends to flick a pinch of fluff
Disdainfully away;
Clare's coat was never such a grey,
Nor of such modish stuff.

And yet, for just a month or so,
Ten years ago, her being slim
And smiling, set my heart askim—
And with that thought sweeps in a flood
Of curious pain, as when the blood
Regarrisons a limb

Or merely, as now, fires a blush
To think how, while the sun ran hay-
Wire through her hair, I lay
Demurely at her side, to trace
Her dusky Cleopatra face
Till pyramids decay—

My very thought, my own cliché...
Ingenuous as I was! But soon
Knew better. She was not to blame
As I recall. I wonder how I came
To call her back to mind? Or met
This tiny rankling of regret,
This milligram of shame?

REVIEWING THE MALVERNS

Here I was childish: this the view I commanded.
Now all the faces are altered: some have unfairly
withdrawn themselves from the sight
of featureless hills, embossed
on the skyline just as I left them;
just as the mind's eye promised,
their long parade.
             But they are dead set
against realignments: now they tell me
they do not take order from me, they are not disposed
to welcome me back, never shared any weakness
for me with those so quickly gone under the weather
that the hills ride out in their old formation,
locked into step like the years,
and the churchyard's rank and file.

A DAY IN THE COUNTRY

Out on one long fingernail of our tentacular town
We avoid the spectacular, don't roll the windows down,
But goggle through glass at a fishy world, and frown
At suspicious strangers.

It might have been safer to visit the City Museum
Where things are properly labelled, and lit by unvarying neon,
Than to venture out by ourselves to the great mausoleum
Where there might be danger

If we stray off the road. Look: those brown things are just like the
                                                        cows in
The kids' farmyard set; what they're doing I think is called browsing—
They seem to inhabit less than substandard housing,
And indulge dirty habits.

But a day in the country helps to supplement reading
And nature is nice, on the whole, though no doubt misleading—
All the squashed rabbits we've scrunched would suggest they've
                                                been breeding
Like rabbits.

Educational, really, I'd call it. The brooklets
Announce correspondence courses in how to run crooked
To a certain goal: and each of these trees' a free booklet
On gracefully aging

Apart from some which are clearly quite dead, and are messing
The whole picture up, like amateur window-dressing.
I came out to worship some nature, but this is depressing,
Like those ruins in Rome.

So, what do you say? I'm sure we'd all be perplexed to
Find value in all this dead stuff, and a little vexed, too.
Say, if we hurry right back we can eat at that neat place right next to
The Funeral Home.

ANTHROPOLOGICAL

There are these people who relished their dream of the Dragon,
chanted eloquent prayers and cast spells, till the dragon came,
gobbled the ones marked out as prime dragon-fodder,
and fell fast asleep. There he lay: they had realized their dream so
                                                              entirely,
they hung by the threads they wove for a dragon to dream.

There was no escape: every route was blocked by the dragon's
slumberous bulk. There were those who wished him away,
chanted eloquent prayers, cast spells for dissolution.
But the fact of him loomed up so large that the simple notion
there might be no dragon was clearly a hopeless delusion—
no dragons in fairy tales: children had dragonless dreams.

Which meant, of course, that everyone slept that much sounder,
and awoke to the fact that the dragon's standard of sleeping
determined their habit of life. It was surely better:
no more loud quarrels, for fear of rousing the dragon;
lest the dragon lose sleep, they conversed in more musical accents;
the dragon served well as a rallying-point of consensus;
they quieted their brats with threats they would waken the dragon.

All this was a good time ago. The dragon still sprawls there.
In his shadow, under the hang of rigorous wings,
is shelter: crops fertilized with his excretions
do well. An atmosphere tinged with sulphur
is the natural air they breathe. They almost embrace the error
of thinking him dead, till his breathing judders and fumes,
as he shifts in his sleep, with a scaly clatter,
or an eyelid totters, a blink of the furnace,
a hellish wink mocking their vision. They blench
when a hot stench blasts them: though they have lost faith
in the ancient spells, and the sonorous chants, they gibber
meaningless things, clawing to cling together
in their sultry night, at the growl of a terminal thunder.

THE LION'S SHARE

The bars, being there, slice lions down to size:
this one was mighty brave to take the air
of wintry London; glum, he stood
regardant on his skimpy field of mud,
and suffered our clear stare
with a prim wincing of uncivil eyes.

We looked around him, smug, and almost bored
by weight of haunch and shoulder, lean
intake of loin, the paws' disarming pudge.
His jaw's hard slant, the bitter lemon wedge
of face seemed merely mean,
seedy, familiar. Till he roared.

Not in grand rage, not raw magniloquence
of appetite; more in the passive voice
of utter boredom: *God, I've been mucked enough*,
said his large grumble as the grudging cough
lurched out of him. And blew the bars
apart, that instant, screamed our common sense

of hearing, in recoil. Not mere loud sound,
the living voice is fleshing-out of breath.
We felt his press on us, the crisp of hair
scorched by his rancor sulphuring the air—
no breathing-space with death
one leap away—and then our weak eyes found
(the bars being there) they were just looking round.

OVERTURE: 1832

(Much detail here is drawn from
Chapter 6 of L. T. C. Rolt's
Isambard Kingdom Brunel.)

Hayfields and gravelpits in Kensington:
the cultured musk twines scent with good cigars
in the walled garden, on midsummer nights
when Felix Mendelssohn
charms the piano in their drawing room
to sketch the harmony of stars,
till, at an upper window, Mamma sets
the tactful beam of her domestic moon
to steer the girls to bed, the young men home.

Consider Fanny as she takes her diary
into her smiling confidence: these gentlemen
with their romantic names!
As yet not even joking dreams of Mary
yielding to Isambard: how could one then
smell, on the still air, more than the stale combustion
of neighbors' hayricks? Times
are not yet prime for smog, urban congestion,
or Church Street winding down to Ponting's, Derry & Tom's

glutted with merchandise from every land
still unsurveyed, ungridded as she scrawls
her doubts of Mr. Brunel's sense of humor.
His brisk footfall
picks out the beat of railroads planned as grand concerti,
sempre accelerando. High above the city,
night's brilliant rivetting: he hears
the world tune up, pitch to that higher key
where he would tap the music of the spheres.

THE BATTLE OF BRITAIN

These beaches are not littered
with unexploded shells;
nothing here to tell
of strife, except a shattered
pillbox, the Martello

tower sunk on the Crumbles.
Vacant, the blue sky overhead,
and trim new roofs the only red
in sight. No cannon mumbles
across the map of meadows

where troops of lumpish cattle
fan to deploy their mood
of conscientious lassitude.
The only smoke of Battle
puffs from Beacon Vista's pseudo-

Tudor chimney-pots. All clear,
far as one sees, the basking hills
return their casualties as nil:
there's no contest here.
On one side, stunted willows

march as a crookleg river winds,
and, here and there, some mildly flustered
crophead greensmocked rustics muster
and straggle into lines
or huddled ambuscadoes—

cut off, demoralized, unmanned.
Through their tattered scrim,
rakish, clean-limbed
pylons strut across the land
with arms akimbo.

SCANT JUSTICE

The General's high-octane breath,
his great grey sigh of a car,
a ghost sweating out his *Memoirs*—
all of these are

luxuries to Maud,
who has a WELCOME mat,
the silver spoon that Nanny left her,
photos of her cat—

luxuries to Bogger,
who has the wind up his sleeve,
the *Financial Times*, a bench by the river,
iced air to breathe—

luxuries to Stavros,
who has lice, weak knees,
a light in the eyes, diminished sexual prospects,
and a lucky bootlace. These

spell luxury, now, to the General:
stern black headlines warn
Maud of a blow to Moderate interests,
and help keep Bogger warm.

VENICE AND THE LOOKING-GLASS

In Venice, in a window, in a mirror—
a lucid stretch of light pooled by its frame
of bosky cherubs plumping for enjoyment—
she caught herself, already caught there. Not
self-seeking, knowingly: it was a shock
to meet herself, at ease, in such a setting.

Hello! she thought, *have you been here for long?*
I hadn't realized we'd been separated.
Where did you get to? It's so easy
to lose oneself completely in this city....
She beamed, and she was beamed on. Suddenly,
she liked the way she looked; she felt she fitted.

And walking, happy, with herself again,
it took no time at all to get quite lost
once more, in Venice, which makes ample room
for absences, reunions, subtle flittings,
the pulse and dance of highlights which its waters
glance up to illustrate a wealth of bridges.

She might have cooed: *I lost my heart to Venice....*
had Venice not restored it, in that moment
when she saw someone in the glass she favored.
No crawler, dying to be wise or witty—
herself, and stepping lively, and content to
grin like a dog and run about that city.

THE ANIMAL-LOVER

Good dog, Argos,
bedded in the shit,
good dog, easy:
can you hear him yet?

Up the beach he crunches,
relishing each stone;
seaworn nostrils pinching
the special salt of home.

Lie quiet, Argos—
running sores and fleas—
dying to infect him,
hatefully diseased.

He wants no commotion:
he's had enough of fighting.
His wife's as chaste as ever:
he might just invite them

to stay a little longer
till they've heard all his tales.
Really, all he wants to do is
flop down like a sail.

Good dog, Argos,
rag and bone and mud.
Good dog, greet him,
change his mind to blood.

When you growled to see them
make themselves at home,
did they try to win
you over with fat bones,

until they came to call you
damned thankless sneaking cur?
Did you choose neglect
eking out the years

until the moment—now—
when he passes by?
Lay back your ears,
judder your rump: his eye

flickers—my dog! Argos!
jerk your rusty tail,
let your last gasp trigger
his colossal kill.

Lie quiet, Argos:
although, at his side,
you may jog no longer,
he will stand supplied

with your old companions:
the bow, the bristling sheaf
of arrows, like a mouthful
of unfailing teeth.

He will draw the bowstring
taut, and deftly—
good dog, Argos—
unleash it, swiftly.

SANSON

Father to son, and son again; our skill
Is sovereign to the State, and surgical.
Crimes breed like maggots, and her body sweats
With disaffection: bad blood must be let.
Your common hangman is a bloated leech,
A more instinctive guzzler, but I teach
My axe the scalpel's business, trim my whip
To pinch the poison out of limbs, or lips.
Treason, sedition run like pus: I lance
The filthy scabs and garboils of sick France.

The fever mounts, as France falls to her knees
And ratches up her lingering disease;
I make no diagnosis, but perform
The proper cautery: sickness has many forms.
They say the land is rotten at the core,
A cancerous crown, the court a running sore
Chafed by its follies—they shall laugh no more:
My lords must curtsey to a raw-boned queen
And I, her consort: *vive la guillotine!*
Successive factions sicken in their place,
And the knife shuttles at a quickening pace.
I wear no favors, serve all men alike,
And I sleep soundest in the land tonight.

And, waking, smile. You fools who catterwaul
And snigger as I rule your carnival:
You shrink if I come close, but I can go
Serene among you, know what you dimly know:
That upon me depends your standing joke.
No Crown, no church? *I* am both King and Pope.
You mayfly men, who take turns to command,
Then come to me to purify the land,
Your blood swills easy from a practiced hand.
Mine is the House that will not be deposed,
And mine the only gentle blood, that flows
Demurely in my veins, and fears no taint
Of mingling with the common coats of paint

That daily daub my altar, and my throne.
Who signs the warrant that will be his own?
I mark him mine, and quickly he appears
To pay the full obeisance of his fear
To me, to me! I only scorn the plague
That blanches all men's faces, runs its rage
Through all Estates, through court and bishopric....
I only will survive. Who dares say I am sick?

THE HORROR MOVIES

for Richard Lindley

"Some Jews, under menace, become Nazi thugs, learn to strut in uniform and beat their fellows. Children sit huddled on the public streets, stick-limbed, dying, their eyes huge and confused. And someone trained a lens on them: always one comes back to that."

—from a review by John Coleman of the film *Requiem for 500,000*, assembled by Jerzy Bossak and Wacław Kaźmierczak from material shot by cameramen of the Wehrmacht, SS, and Gestapo: *New Statesman*, 25 December 1964.

I fear this instrument
Of moral anaesthetic:
One moistureless dark eye,
Transfixing the event,
Its fixative applies:
An inhumane aesthetic.

The filming coldness seeps
Back to the eye, the hand
That regulates, depresses—
What else is it possesses
The man to squint, adjust his stand,
When he might turn away and weep?

—To see a boy burst into fire,
Ricepaper skin peel off in strips;
A woman carefully inspects
The crawling sky: the lens admires
Her child, asprawl, and on whose lips
A beady fly prospects.

And you, whose bland well-nurtured rumps
Plump out your plushy seats:
Disregard perspective,
Don't tell me of technique.
The cutting is effective?
The pans are running jumps

At what men have to live for
If we are not to freeze
Into cool, observant
Precision instruments
Of Art for Art's sake, please...
O Jesus, what I'd give for

Some straying out of focus,
Some small home-movie goof;
Better, the fine edge of strain
Lacing precision: proof
That what whirs like a locust
Is not man, but machine.

Or just an artless lecture
Furious enough for art:
Look here, upon this picture,
And turn and look on these,
The view of *War's Disasters*
That devastates the heart.

Francisco Goya fecit—
The formal phrase confines
The passion gone to make it,
The discipline that kept
Blood from slubbering the lines
His raging pencil mapped.

On each, the mind that mocked at,
Cursed, tasted what it drew,
Speaks out: the titles cryptic:
These too. So much and more.
The words are plain and few:
This is not to be looked at
Is hard by *This I saw.*

MRS. SCHMIDT TALKS ABOUT POLLUTION

You couldn't ever hang the wash outside:
The wind would blow our way. My Heinrich's cuffs,
All nice and white, got blackened with the stuff
Before he'd been an hour at work. We tried
To keep things decent, always took a pride
In our appearances, but just a puff
Of air would make us smutty. Like black fluff,
But sort of greasy, too: it never dried
But smeared our hands—the devil to get clean.
And this new soap we tried just made things worse.
Gritty, it was, and never lathered rightly.
Funny to think of now, of course: it's been
So long since then, but oh dear, what a curse—
Living near Dachau, back in forty-three.

FREEZING LEVEL

Outside, the snow has stopped: the final few
fritillaries have wavered down, and now
the stars confirm a quiet and compound freezing.
The world's turned scholarly,
its dirty habits not to be supposed
for the duration.
Only the distantly demented wheezing
of some fool's car that's dying on the hill
sustains a vulgar sense of civilization.

Indoors, the music glints: the lovely light
artillery of Mozart concentrates
our fire's loose structures into dazzling
salons and galleries
which blaze and buckle, yet remain composed
for the duration.
Only your scent, silk's rustle, sudden bristling
of skin that grazes skin make me recall
a lucid précis lives in limitation:
we lose ourselves in placid meditation.

Next morning's thaw returns the roads to slush,
buttery sunlight, bitter tangs of ash,
fat milksop clouds across the scoured sky dawdling,
life's charge and battery
renewed. Once more, the world's disposed,
for its duration,
to muck and muddle. The radio bubbles maudlin
lovers' farewells. And we're not in the mood
for crystal or cadenzas, constellations

nailed down by order. Strain to inflict
slavery on the stars, but blink, and space is flecked
with random sparks again. We seek control in
gracious forms, but more such silvery
harmonic nights could freeze our hearts, impose
on them mere fabrications.
Welcome again, dreck, flotsam, junkyard, sprawling
limbs of life, of love, of steaming trees
nodding their heads,
shedding the weight of brilliant condensation.

MISTRAL

for Donald Davie

"The poet falls to special pleading, chilled
To find in Art no fellow but the wind."

Davie: "The Wind at Penistone"

Provence equates
Her poet with a wind, which frets
The trees lop-sided, cultivates
The peasants' rancor, sets
Their nerves, and teeth, on edge.

This sounds more like the truth
Than talk of potent form, a popular voice
Which "legislates,"
But leaves one little choice
(Beyond sour grapes)

Except to live, man among men,
And only whet one's tongue to praise
The generous spirit's evidence
Of love for anything well made
And making sense.

And, when one comes to speak, to fan
One's words into a local breeze
So mastered, figured, and refined
It stirs the very few, who mind
Not what it does, but is.

A DIM VIEW

They may whistle for tribute soon:
the last Master will be dead.
We shall see no-one
notably striding ahead.

That should make the going easy—
this dogged itch to run
till we catch up to them:
how shall we move when that's gone?

No more great figures,
only inflated zeroes.
Young pretenders in place of the grand old men.
Contemporaries, no heroes.

and it came to an end. Someone plucked
at his sleeve, and pointed. He looked round
and saw them all clapping.
The clowns!
All squeezing invisible concertinas,
the mime so absurd the sense of such wheezing
made his eyes buzz. All out of time:
black elbow-vents
flapped in the breeze, shot rippling dents
through stiff shirt-fronts. Black velvet breasts
rhythmically pressed
and cleaving asunder; some smacked a hand
down into the other, some hit up from under,
some patted butter.
Look at that girl with her arms in a stutter,
and her sister trying to trap a
moth in her gloves; their mother
over and over at prayer. So many pairs
of pincers and clappers
and still going on! See that dapper
young fellow wincingly tapping
his palms into shape, and his neighbor, slapping
his almost to pulp, and that one persisting
in sketching the bulk of the fish he just missed! In-
sane! It should make him madly
incensed with such asses, if he didn't feel, oddly,
hand-in-hand with the crowd...

And at last, as (in quite
the right style) he bowed,
he could hear himself starting to smile.

MORAL CONCLUSIONS

As he laye unravelling in the agonie of death, the Standers-
by could hear him say softly, "I have seen the Glories of the
world."
>   —*Aubrey's Brief Lives*: Isaac Barrow.

I work at endings to make endings work:
Poems that finish with "a click
like a box closing" is the trick I seek.

A life should end as well. I keep a store
of grand finales: Raleigh's, or Voltaire
lighting on words to cap the striking hour

with one last stroke of wit. Was it just luck
that prompted him to an immortal joke?
Or could it be a lifetime of technique

renders one prone to happy accident?
Can we maintain a discipline that won't
let us conclude in chaos, or in cant?

May we assume a habit of good talk
won't let us die of *grand mal d'esthétique*?
Brave words, where are you when the voice must break?

Will you stand by us at the last, demanding
that our last pinch of mortal understanding
should rouse our speech to make a decent ending?

I grant you that this tone's unsympathetic:
a rigid form, no welter of exotic
images, questions that prove didactic

are none of them in fashion. Nor is saying
that fashion takes short views, and shies from seeing
the Glories of the world. Neither is dying:

unravelling in agonie. The man is sick?
No pun in Aubrey's title? Mere rhetoric?
Thank God for anaesthesia? Heretic,

if I were reading this to you, aloud,
you might be sure I schemed it to provide
a good ill-favored moral to conclude

the evening's entertainment. Look,
we've travelled no great distance by the clock
towards the final box's formal click,

putting full-stop to all we choose to speak.

THE CHECK-UP

Submissive to the doctor's will
I lay my watch down on the window-sill
And poke a limp hand forward. Time stands still

And holds my breath up as his fingers clutch;
Credulous, huddled in its shaky hutch,
Heart flinches from the cold professional touch—

Dud? Dud?
—And then the ignorant swagger of my blood
Perks up against his thumb; that liquid thud

Is regular as clockwork, lets me be
Myself again. "Good for a lifetime," he
Concludes; that tone of comic sympathy

Is made to measure; yes, he has the trick.
He turns to wash his hands. Well, that was quick.
And on my wrist again the tick tick tick.

SNOW DADDY

Her snowman sports his shabbiest hat; she squeaks
piercingly as she jabs
a pipe he used to own
his favorite, roughly where the mouth would be
if he had ways to speak.
For eyes, she picks out two black shiny stones.

And now she chatters down his weak
demurs at the resemblance
that she insists on, and will dance
around the solemn buffer who conforms
to what her fancy wishes, till she must
submit to being fed, and loved, and warm

once she has changed. And then, how soon
only a greying lumpishness remains
blobbing the caustic green, and every day
shrinks more into itself, and out of sight
of her concerns. At last, the rain
has whittled all but two small stones away.

FINAL DIRECTIONS

I hate a tended grave. Save me a place
to go to seed in, growing so absorbed
some craft beyond a common practice shapes
my plot and has me, breathless, utter
what comes most natural. There's a point
where skillful trimming is the work of hacks:
death should be one word no-one can compose
neat settings for. With life ruled out at last
it's time to wax romantic, and go dead.

If there's a stone, I want that soon to sag,
lurch in the fetters ivy loops about it,
relinquish all distinction. I trust the various weather,
lichen, and snail make epitaph a cipher,
and name a blank. I hope the fat
swags of rank grass, weeds bogged in succulence
thrive on what contributions I submit
to snag and ramble: let extravagance
brag in green garbled tongues that they compound
and bring to light what I could not account for:
slips of the tongue, jetsam of dreams, stray tags
of nonsense rhymes, the potpourri of fancies
a lifetime's editing rightly rejected.

I want my bones' allotment to run mad: that small
cloudburst of wilderness tell the passer-by
no more of me than, when I came to die,
confusion was my style: I lost control.

A STAGE OF DEVELOPMENT

Matthew Henson, Commander Robert Peary's black servant,
raised the U.S. flag at the North Pole, April 1909.

Right on the nose of the Pole
Peary's nigger breaks out the flag.
In the middle of nowhere someone
Shakes out a rag.

Blotting the spotless canvas
A hooligan smudge of burnt cork.
Against the blackboard the teacher's
Face flares out like chalk.

A chimneysweep soiling the linen.
A snowman stuck in the coal.
Turning the country upside down.
Giving the nation its soul.

Positive action, and now.
Negative: stop or we shoot.
Something is blowing in here:
It could be detergent. Or soot.

MORE NOBLE DUST

The original codex, which according to a venerable tradition was discovered wedging a wine barrel in Verona, at the end of the thirteenth century A.D., was in a poor state. There were frequent *lacunae* in the text, attributable (according to the same tradition) to the operation of the wine on the parchment. Worse than this, the codex itself disappeared again as mysteriously as it had appeared, although fortunately not before at least two copies had been taken.

> —from the introduction to *The Poems of Catullus*, translated by Peter Whigham.

How you would smile, Catullus, at this
typical flick of your own witty insolence,
if you knew that, in time,
Time's wry sense of what's fitting would screw
up your words, in one ball,
to sphincter the asshole of an old barrel
and sop up its swills
of *vin ordinaire*, in decaying Verona,

and laugh at the scholarly pickle that issues
out of the wodge of soggy papyrus
at long last uncorked.
Deploring a codex foxed with chianti
and the flagrant bouquet
of indelicate Eros, a corps of dry cleaners
laced the lacunae
of Lesbia's panties, made shifts for graffiti,

lamented the blotches an immodest time
and wine's operation inflicted. But what
of the waste of the drink
that wasted the words, yet in turn took a tincture
of spirit from song?
Did that rough *paesano* admit a refinement,
fine palates detect
a lyrical tinge, strain of carmine in rouge?

Who stayed at the inn? Did staid Veronesi
stop for a glass, start frisking the maids?
Was the priest there unfrocked?
Did the girls snatch their skirts, did toper and tenor
vie for snatches of song
and find their tongues twisting to liquorish Latin?
And what of the lovers,
lost and belated, looking for shelter

and sober repose, who then couldn't sleep,
but frolicked the night out, shaking the bed—
partly with laughter—
at feeling their limbs pressed to sensual inventions,
matching carols of lust?
Were the artists there lively? Was life then an art
as easy as drinking?
Did their poems infuse that life they were steeped in

before the cork popped? Lees of that vintage
wrinkle the dust; to dust crinkled
the poetry—dry, you may say.
Do you really drink vinegar? Read for a stopgap?
Chew on dry corks?
How you would laugh, if you could, at Catullus,
who made only songs
good for centuries, for stopping a bung-
hole; mouthfuls of living
in a dead tongue.

TEMPORA MUTANTUR...

How stale, flat, unprofitable, etcetera;
'Tis an unweeded garden.
Pantyhose no hard-on
Provoke: once it was better.

Once we were fifteen,
Our flesh blissfully martyred
By the quick flash of black garter,
Girls angling their seams.

That lust's all gone to seed;
The sprigs of first impression
Woefully out of fashion:
We must be our age, indeed.

My first love thought maturity
Her first bra: just a halter
My new girl wears. Times alter:
In some ways, so do we;
A little, grudgingly.

IN EXTENUATION

Mankind on trial: yes, it might melt the stones
to hear poor Nature's tales of rape and sack,
the tears wrung from her since we relish salt.
We lay our belt across Alaska's back?
Guilty. But, Sir, we have our own
petitioners to call before Your court.
There's Florence, caked with mud above her knees;
how long can Venice stand the lickerish sea's
unbridled fingers plucking at her skirts?
Is the next earthquake San Francisco's fault?

MISTER MAN

Mister! they yell, and then, still sharper, *Mister!*
and bring me down to earth. Rough grass, and mud.
What can they...? Oh. Get on the ball:
bounce, soggy bounce, hop-toad, rolls dead
a yard away. They all fall silent. Watch me.
Dunlop to take the penalty. In his best shoes?
Oh well. And oh, how well it feels:
punching it square and soundly, grooving out
a long inch-perfect cross to that fair boy
whose hands snap off his hips, who traps it cleanly,
veers, pulls all eyes his way. They might say thanks?
But *Bill!* they scream—*here, Bill! Bill, pass!* and stream
towards the distant goal. Damn it: a smear
on my new YoungLook slacks: lucky I didn't go
arse over tip. *Pass, Bill, you idiot:*
get rid of it. Ah, Bill, you held too long.
One thin voice, woeful, shrieks, *Oh, bad luck, Bill!*—
was that the one who needled, *Come ON, Mister?*
I think one little prick squeaked, *Chuck it, Pop.*

SUCH SMALL DEER

Old photographs perplex:
We cannot quite conceive
Those blooming, faded children
Could pass for us, nor quite retrieve

What are, for us, still lives. I see
My namesake, with a toy
Bear nuzzling his ear: what
Secrets can they enjoy?

We work up smiles to see ourselves
Laughing, at play. But never
In kids at *Happy Families*
Quite comprehend ourselves, each other,

Or sister, perched on Brownie,
Faint ink: *May '48.*
We recognize the animal
(The girl's quite out of date)

And view, with more affection
Than for our past, the pets
Who show up here and there, and seem
Somehow, more real. And yet—

How obvious, how the obvious shocks!—
How dead they are. Old Java:
Even his great-grandkittens now
Are gathered to their fathers.

Or rather, if one trace remains
Of Ptolemy, or Tigger,
Or Tigger's kittens, one might light
Somewhere on a sliver

Of fraying bone, or even
A flat barbaric skull,
Snarling, picked clean, and packed with dirt;
Not sleek nor strokeable

But indescribably remote
From nursery illustrations
Of loving animals...I think
Of small beasts' skeletons,

The cunning of the linked and locked
Interdependence, filigree-
work of vertebrae,
Breathless fragility

—Something I first saw as a child:
The child these snapshots claim, that must
Blanch, dwindle, grow still more delicate,
Whitening into dust.

WAKING

Benign, familiarly unreal
As a child's home, my dream
So spaciously reveals
That landscape, still serene—

But waking: an explosion!
Ejected with such force
It cracks the rifled chambers,
I smash into myself

And should be spinning, flying,
Leapfrogging with the stars—
Slow, like a frizzled spider,
I painfully contract

Into the workaday dimension
Self-consciousness incurs;
My shocked hand recognizes
My cheek debauched with tears.

I lie here, still, but shaky;
The bottle of myself
So cruelly agitated
The stopper should blow off....

Slowly things group around me:
Things should be as they are.
The alien breath beside me
Becomes familiar.

More alien and more visionary
Those sights, as my sight clears;
And flatter and remoter
That singing in my ears.

I heave my body out of bed,
Cough briefly, lurch my way
To coffee drunk, newspaper read,
Dog let out to play.

WALKING THE DOG

Sick of the tetchy, intermittent scolds
my flesh and blood emits from its deep cot,
sick of the hot
preposterous impotence
that scalds my throat, but leaves her grace quite cold,
until I half-admire the fine, controlled
achievement of her flaming nonchalance—
the bitch can make a six-month-old
New Yorker yield her fresh intelligence—
sick of the lot,
I snatch, plume, whistle up
my coat, intention, almost full-grown pup.

Outside, it's dark: frost
edges the air.
I mark the sudden prick
of the dog's ears, and thrust
of his contentious muzzle, swear
correctly at him—but I nearly sic
him onto pussy where
she freezes, hunched, malevolent.
How I could envy him that quick
and finished sense
of unresolvable difference!
"Good boy," I mutter, easier on the chain:
I take back 'bitch,' again.

The farthest houses sink behind us:
I snap him free—
he lunges off, interrogates a tree,
then, in the easy, fluent, mindless
flush of his long-legged ecstasy,
sweeps round in circles of pure running,
until I catch the trick, beginning
to sprint, swerve, dodge as he comes bombing
in, like a young typhoon....
We sprawl together in the damp deep grass;
grabbing for breath and laughter, his warm tongue at my face,
I shake my heels at the moon.

OLD TOM

First—just a kit—a boot squelched him,
voided his screeching innards.
Then a charged flex had him reeling,
salted his whiskers
with a fizzy icing.

Once he was drowned
though he scrabbled his ratty scrawn
out of the rainbutt, polished it off
licking the rest of his lives into shape.
Once he was stoned

by dead-end kids ganged for a killing:
he laid down his ears and scarpered
like a wink of spit off a shovel,
and counted his breaks on the rooftop.
Next, he took poison

neat from the garbage's delicatessen:
by jerks, he coughed up a lifetime
of hairballs and rotgut gobbets.
Once a tussle of yipsnapper mongrels
had him worried to death.

Once he was hanged if the clinching crook of a tree
couldn't bear him to cling to his freezing.
And once, in a yowling rut up the alley,
sharpslashers nailed him, scraped on his throatstrings,
clipped off an ear by their scoring.

Now he considers chances,
thinning his longshot eyes, switching
a nibble of tail at the odds.
He reckons his claws in, and purrs: eight down,
the hell of a tough one to go.

A CLASSIC CASE

Be careful, rooting in the basement,
what you dislodge there. Look,
don't say *these spiders are a perfect menace*,
but mind that box of books: *Alice*,
Lear, Grimm...spines stamped with gilt will catch
the eye: they tug you back
and pin you. Ragged bindings latch
on to your hands: before you know, you're hooked.
Is it dim light down there sets you to spell
the sense out? Was it that rusted nail
that pricked out liquid beads along your arm?
What *is* that sticky stuff you can't brush free from?

Get back to business, innocent adult reading:
normal enough, as all the experts vouch.
Down at the inky bottom of the well
lies poor Brer Rabbit, on Brer Fox's couch,
crying, and pleading
(and now with no false panic in his squeal):
Doctor, do anything but that!
Don't throw me back
into that briarpatch, that knot of thorns
and love-lies-bleeding,
where everything that's wrong was born,
and goes on breeding.

SUNSTRUCK

Pinned down by sun, spread-eagled,
I watch my eyelids, veined
Like grapes, thin-skinned, and changing
Under my press, from fine
Vermilion into red arterial
Roads all running wine.

Heat holds me in a truss
That reaffirms my bones.
Around my limp fist, sand
Fashions a grainy cestus;
Open and hardened, I am honeycombed
Like pumicestone.

Drowsy, I hear the sea:
It simplifies my head
Into a dusky, brimming
Cupola of bronze.
Only my belly, like a sponge,
Gluttonous, swollen,

Knows none of this refinement,
Plumps for the cool of dark,
Moon like a slice of citron,
Owls in the myrtle-grove,
Hands' questioning, silk's sibilance,
And the long squeeze of love.

In the hot mosaic
Sun prints upon my blindness,
I figure brilliant children—
Gold skins, and eyes like sloes—
One with a net and trident,
One with a golden bow.

LESSONS ON THE LAWN

Squirrels will never learn, insist
on treating serious humanists

with active, unconcealed suspicion.
To make them query their tradition,

pacifically I offered one
part of an old and nasty bun,

and wore my pal-to-squirrels grin.
Across the grass he skeetered, in

a series of electric shocks:
tail flexed, pop-eyed, he stopped to box

the air, as signal I should lob
what I might have to stop his gob

and, when it fell six inches short,
he glared, and quivered; sniffed, and thought,

and made a dash for it, and bolted
booty in cheek. I felt insulted

by his off-hand manipulation.
Squirrels lack discrimination,

where we distinguish. Proof: I wouldn't
dispense stale crumbs to bug-eyed students.

SQUARE

is what you may call me, and welcome.
Should I be ashamed
that the trendy patter would place me
in a pride of resonant names?
Quadrangle, cloister, piazza,
the marketplace—
wherever men like to be serious, or need to
develop a sensible space,
they tend toward squares; of all games
the purest is checkered: giving
reason to pastime, and logic its music, is,
by definition, living.

In a pure state of Nature,
squares may not exist, but for man
to shape his life by right angles
is natural enough; he can
neither improve upon Nature, nor live by
her crazy directions. He may only create
alternatives, ordered constructions,
a pattern becoming his state.
She squiggles and doodles, at best she
describes perfect circles, like sun
that warms the carved stone, illuminates squares that attest to
the good sense of man.

Some squares are more shapely than others:
I hope to be one
that gathers the sunlight, and offers
relief from the sun.
With room for diversion, yet ever
a center of craft, and fair trade,
and even my shadier sides maintaining
a decent façade.
Let me be wrought into balance, my lines
discover perspective, amounting
to more than the sum of my parts.
Set in the middle, performing its function, a fountain.

A LITTLE EPITHALAMIUM

for Tom and Dana

Each day's a place to move in; some
with living-room too meager
or, frankly, ruinous.
Others are lighter, brighter, bigger,
and you're at large, at home
in a fine open house
friends find welcome.

May this day be one
Time's spyglass loves to dwell on,
spot where familiar treasure
once was a new belonging. Still, on
dwindling windows may the sun
spark dazzling recollection
of here-and-now; your happiness, our pleasure.

CARUSO FOR THE CHILDREN

"Listen," I tell my children, "Listen...."
but they look blank.
I cannot force my love upon them: disson-
ance comes of that.

Nor teach them how to live: breathing
remains a lonely art.
Fathers, as well as tenors, fear
strains of the unaccompanied heart.

They play with dolls, and cars,
under the aerial span
of aria, expanding: *Ah*
la paterna mano....Man

needs a diversity of love
to train his voice to giving
what children need to hear. At night,
to study their soft breathing,

I stand by their dark beds as rapt
as if that quiet recitative
were of my composition, shaped
by this preserving voice that gives

so prodigal, of living art,
I think they cannot choose but hear
what I might tell them, pointlessly:
how each note weights the air

as shapely as the globe of glass
blown into contour, yet
veined with the blood's warm inspiration,
heady, exsufflicate,

as round and ripe as the good fruit
on the swayed, laden boughs
of trees of expert grafting, craft
and nature married; how

still he proposes, fifty
years since his death,
this paradoxically unthrifty
controlled expenditure of breath.

Notes:

Above It All: page 36, line 17: Mizoguchi's *Ugetsu Monogatari*.

The Battle of Britain: page 44, lines 5-6, 14-16: Martello towers were built in anticipation of invasion during the Napoleonic wars. The Crumbles is a sandspit running into the English Channel near Eastbourne. Battle is a village near Pevensey, the site of the Battle of Hastings. Beacons were lit to warn of the approach of the Spanish Armada.

Caruso for the Children: page 80, lines 11-12: Macduff's aria in Verdi's *Macbeth*, and one of Caruso's finest recordings.

A Change of Mood: page 33, line 17:
humbug:
(1) claptrap, nonsense
(2) a large, zebra-striped peppermint candy.

End of Summer: page 20: Yasujiro Ozu, the great film director.

A Face in the Crowd: page 38, line 24: a romantic convention, inadvertently similar to line 6, Poem *946*, by Emily Dickinson.

Midland Autumn: page 6, line 25: Imitation poppies are sold and worn in November to commemorate Armistice Day, 1918.

Mistral: page 56:
(1) A cold, dry, northerly wind of the Mediterranean provinces of France.
(2) Frédéric Mistral (1830-1914): Provençal poet; received the Nobel Prize for Literature in 1904.

Overture 1832: page 43, line 18: Ponting's and Derry & Tom's: renowned, but (*sic transit*) now departed department stores in Kensington.

Sanson: page 49: Charles-Henri Sanson (1739-1795?), from a long family line of executioners, served as official executioner in Paris during the French Revolution.

Scant Justice: page 45: Report in London has it that those reduced to sleeping outdoors, swaddled in newspaper to keep off the cold, find that the *Financial Times* provides the best insulation.

Wimborne Minster: page 4, line 8: A fox's *mask* is a preserved fox's head, occasionally used for interior decoration after the manner of stag's heads and other trophies.

•

William Dunlop was born at Southampton, England. He received his education at Eastbourne College, with the Gordon Highlanders, and at Queens' College, Cambridge, where he edited the magazine *Granta*. In 1962 he came to Seattle to work with Theodore Roethke. He is an Associate Professor of English at the University of Washington, and for many years was soccer correspondent and opera critic for the *Seattle Weekly*. He is married, with three children, and lives in Seattle.